Angela Craig is a passionate pioneer in the world of online ministry. When Angela left my office to plant an online church, I watched in amazement as Jesus used her to reach thousands in just a few months. Listen to her advice and follow it and you'll do well.

DON ROSS
Author of *Turnaround Pastor*; superintendent, NWMN of the Assemblies of God

Angela Craig is like many talented individuals attending church who are gifted and have a dream. The only thing they need is someone who will believe in them and an opportunity. Angela was given an opportunity to plant the first online church in our organization and has excelled far beyond what I imagined.

DAVE COLE
Author of *What the Church Can Learn From Harley-Davidson;* assistant superintendent, NWMN of the Assemblies of God

ONLINE JESUS

A Guide to Community, Discipleship, & Care Online

By
Angela Lynne Craig

Online Jesus: A Guide to Building Community, Disciple & Care Online
By Angela Lynne Craig

For my PCL family…

CONTENTS

INTRODUCTION..9

PART I: COMMUNITY 13

PART II: DISCIPLE 41

PART III: CARE..53

PART IV: PRACTICAL TIPS FOR CHURCH ONLINE ..65

EPILOGUE...77

NOTES 81

ABOUT THE AUTHOR..................................85

INTRODUCTION

"Unless you act when it feels too early, it's actually too late."[1] Many leaders have felt the weight of this statement since the outbreak of the novel coronavirus. Maybe that leader is you. With church doors closed in the interest of public health, we are faced with the question: What now?

You might feel overwhelmed thinking of all the questions that need answers: How do we create community online? How do we effectively disciple? How do we care for people when we can't see them? How do we teach, take communion, or baptize new believers? Do we hold out until the storm passes? What if, when the church reopens, people stay home and continue to watch church online like their favorite Netflix show? If we do go online, where will I find the time, money, and people to start something new? There are so many questions you may be asking in the wake of this pandemic that has upended life, as we know it.

These were some of the same questions I asked myself over six years ago, before I started my first online group on Facebook. I wrestled with the overarching question: How do we create community, disciple, and care online? In 2017, we launched the first social media church approved by the Assemblies of God. Today, using Facebook as our main platform, Pursuit Church Live serves more than 14,000 people in 45 countries, speaking 43 different languages.

I believe God has prepared you to lean in and step up "for such a time as this" (Esther 4:14). Now, more than ever, the church has unparalleled potential and opportunity to bring the hope of Jesus to our communities and ignite our imagination of what the church can be. According to Pew Research Center, in April 2019, roughly 7 in 10 adults throughout the U.S. were on social media each month.[2] Facebook, the leading social platform, had 2.45 billion monthly active users and 1.62 billion daily users.[3] Today, with most businesses closed and people at home, digital attention has reached an unprecedented all-time high. Facebook reports that overall U.S. traffic from Facebook to other websites has increased by more than 50% week-on-week.[4]

In this book, your will find many reasons for your church to engage in digital ministry, but let me start with 43,000. Forty-three thousand is the number of people who gave their lives to Jesus when over 700 new churches went live for the first time on the Church Online Streaming Platform.[5] And this doesn't even count the multitude of other streaming platforms, like Facebook and YouTube.

The opportunity to build God's kingdom online every day is enormous. Not only can online church be the front door to faith for millions, your church can be the lifeline to Jesus for your members and local community during this time of world crisis. Imagine how different the world would be if the hope and love of God permeated every post, every video, and every online chat.

Now is time to take a deep breath and focus and remember we are in this together.

> Then Jesus came to them and said, "All authority in heaven and on earth has been given to me. Therefore, go and make disciples of all nations, baptizing them in the name of the Father and of the Son and of the Holy Spirit, and teaching them to obey everything I have commanded you. And surely I am with you always, to the very end of the age."
> MATTHEW 28:18-20

Welcome to the world of digital ministry.

A note to the reader: The technology we know today will change tomorrow. Although I provide helpful tools in Part 4 of this book, "Practical Tips for Church Online," I recommend and encourage you to make your favorite search engine your friend for step-by-step technical tutorials on specific topics.

PART I:

COMMUNITY

They devoted themselves to the apostles' teaching and to fellowship, to the breaking of bread, and to prayer. Everyone was filled with awe at the many wonders and signs performed by the apostles. All the believers were together and had everything in common. They sold property and possessions to give to anyone who had need. Every day they continued to meet together in the temple courts. They broke bread in their homes and ate together with glad and sincere hearts, praising God and enjoying the favor of all the people. And the Lord added to their number daily those who were being saved.

ACTS 2:42-47, NIV

A church without walls

"Whether in caves, cathedrals or computers, the body of Christ still gathers." —Unknown

Many leaders believe the only place Christian community can be created is inside the four walls of a church building. The example of the early church opens our eyes to other possibilities. We know from reading the scriptures and early historical documents that Christians gathered in the temple, in homes, and wherever they could.

Courtroom testimony in Italy provides a glimpse into the meeting place of the early Christians who lived in a time of persecution, 165 years after Jesus' crucifixion. Rusticus, the

Roman prefect, interrogated one of the most important Greek philosophers in the early Christian church, St Justin Martyr, along with his associates in the trial of their death:

"Where do you assemble?" Rusticus proceeded.

"Wherever we want to and are able to," Justin replied. "Do you imagine that we all meet in the same place? Not so! The God of the Christians is not limited to a location. He is invisible, and he fills heaven and earth. Therefore, he is worshipped and glorified everywhere by the faithful."

Rusticus sighed... "Just tell me where you personally assemble. In other words, in what place do you, Justin, gather your followers?"

...[Justin] continued, "During the entire time I've lived here...I've simply taught the truth to anyone willing to come to me."[1]

The church has been adapting the way they build community and perform important functions for over 2000 years. They did whatever it took to fulfill God's commandments to love others and reach the world with the Good News. To move forward, we need to employ adaptive leadership with that same heart.

My Facebook friend and social media expert, Randall Greene, beautifully encapsulates the need for adaptive leadership in this quote:

"You can't have a real story unless you hear it told."
But then there was written language.

"You can't have a real book unless it's scribed by hand."
But then there was a printing press.

"You can't have a store unless it's brick-and-mortar."
But then there was ecommerce.

Our world is continually evolving, and we ought to embrace those changes in order to help the society of tomorrow look more like Christ, rather than letting the world create tomorrow's society in its own image.

The Early Church didn't have the privilege or freedom to gather in buildings. Instead, people came together wherever they could. Today people are coming together on social media.

Real community exists online

And let us consider how we may spur one another on toward love and good deeds, not giving up meeting together, as some are in the habit of doing, but encouraging one another—and all the more as you see the Day approaching.
HEBREWS 10:24-25

Hundreds of times I have been asked, "Is it possible to create 'real' community online?"

Social media brings people together. So does the Church. That synonymous aim sets the groundwork for a great working relationship between churches and social networks like Facebook, Instagram, and WhatsApp. Not only will church online keep your current members connected, it will serve as the front porch to faith for those on the outside, looking in.

Prior to leading Pursuit Church Live, I was a director at the AG Northwest Ministry Network in Snoqualmie, Washington. Our mission was to develop and strengthen leaders in our 340 network churches. I did this both in person and online.

It was in our women's Facebook groups that I witnessed the power of social networks to bring people together into authentic community. This was surprising and unexpected. I had always believed that "real" relationships were forged in person. Apparently, I was wrong.

These social networks gave women the chance to connect organically, building community around common interests and mutual care. Coming together every day made space and time for women to be heard and their hearts to be seen. It was an environment that moved women from hesitant and vulnerable strangers to authentic and trusted friends. What surprised me most was the number of women who wanted to join our group who did not attend one of our AG churches — or any church. These women were seeking faith, connection, and purpose, and our online groups gave them a safe place to discover all three.

"Our souls crave intimacy"—Erwin Raphael McManus

Think, for a minute, about a person's first time in church. What is it like to walk through the doors of a church where you know no one? What if you are divorced, homeless, single, homosexual, a widow, or struggling with your sexual identity? What if you are a young, single black woman, and the only churches in your area are filled with white middle-class families? Having your church online flattens the hierarchy. It gives people the opportunity to see what your community is about without the perceived risk of rejection or shame that most new attendees anticipate when they think of walking through the front doors of your church.

Now think, for a minute, about those who don't have any local church they can attend.

In the first month after the launch of Pursuit Church Live, my family was on a weekend camping trip to celebrate my birthday. My husband organized a kayak tour that landed, halfway through the paddle, at an island bay filled with oysters. Everyone brought a picnic lunch to share on the beach. It was there that I met Debbie. She was on the kayak tour alone so we invited her to sit with us. As we got to know each other, Debbie shared that she was living in the area and serving as a caregiver for a friend. The town she lived in had no more than a corner grocery store and an abandoned community center. She had been living there for 18 months without any friends or community outside of the person she cared for six days a week. We talked the entire way back to where our cars were parked. When she asked what I did, I had the opportunity to share PCL with her. Before we left each other, I asked if I could pray with her. When we were done, we exchanged phone numbers, and I showed her how to find Pursuit Church Live on Facebook.

The very next week, Debbie joined me on Facebook Live. PCL became Debbie's lifeline to Jesus and to community. It wasn't long before she gave her life to Jesus. Now, Debbie is living back in her hometown and attending and serving at her local church. If I was the pastor of a brick-and-motor church in my town, I never could have invited Debbie to church. At the time, I felt God might have had me start a Facebook church just for Debbie. Now, hundreds of "Debbies" later, I know it is true, without a doubt.

Last fall, I received a message from a PCL member wanting to share a testimony. Cathy, who lives in Texas, had met a Washington woman named Mary in one of our Facebook Bible study groups. Neither woman attended a local church. The two had a lot in common and exchanged phone numbers. Over time, they became long-distance friends, talking on the phone weekly.

This past summer, Mary became ill. She was housebound and alone. Cathy told Mary she wished she could travel to Washington to help, but she didn't have the money. The two women agreed to pray for God to provide the money for a plane ticket. That week, another friend of Cathy's was at her house for Bible study and prayer. As the friend prepared to leave, she said, "Wait a minute! God is telling me to write you a check." The woman wrote Cathy a check for $600 — almost exactly enough to cover a plane ticket with tax! Cathy was able to spend a week with Mary, caring for her. The women prayed together, read the Bible, attended online church, and took communion together. When Cathy returned to Texas, she posted several videos of the great work God had done in their lives during this visit.

God brought hope and healing to both women and increased their faith. Thousands of people have since watched these videos on Cathy's Facebook page and witnessed the greatness of what God can do to change lives through Christian community.

The local church was, and still is, God's plan for Christian community. God created every person with a need to know Him and a desire to be part of a meaningful community. Today, technology can help us create deeper connections and community while ministering to those who might otherwise remain beyond our reach.

The secret to creating community

"To be fully seen by somebody, then, and be loved anyhow - this is a human offering that can border on miraculous."
—Elizabeth Gilbert

Recognition is the most valuable tool you and I have for building an online community. We all come into the world looking for someone who looks for us, someone who sees us, someone who is a witness to our soul.

When our oldest son, Austin, was around six months old, he would sit on the bathroom counter while I got ready. Austin was enamored with the cute baby he saw reflected in the mirror. They exchanged smiles, giggles, a wave hello, and even kisses. In Austin's mind, the baby in the mirror was perfect: no flaw, no shame, and no self-doubt.

In Genesis 1, God said, "Let us make mankind in our image, in our likeness, so that they may rule over the fish in the sea and the birds in the sky, over the livestock and all the wild animals, and over all the creatures that move along the ground. So God created mankind in his own image, in the image of God he created them; male and female he created them" (Genesis 1:26-27).

What Austin saw was his reflection in God. He saw someone looking back at him with unconditional love and acceptance. Something interesting begins to happen after the age of two. When you place a child in front of a mirror, the child no longer engages with his or her perfect image. The child becomes "others focused" and will wait to be engaged by another person before responding to the reflection.[2] Our identity begins to be formed by how we perceive ourselves through the eyes of others. That can be both positive and negative. But, more often than not, our broken world introduces shame, sin, and comparison, erasing any memory of the delighted child who once sat in front of the mirror. Our souls long for the days when we felt wholly loved, accepted, and seen by God and by others.

This is one of the biggest reasons social networks thrive. We post in the hopes someone will tell us our life matters. We post to be seen. There is more to a selfie than showing our friends and family who we are hanging out with or where we have been. Selfies are more than a form of self-expression. They are a call for recognition. Like the child in the mirror, we all want to be seen.

Think of the ways God has interacted with his people throughout history and scripture.

He pursued the hopeless.

Despised and mistreated by her mistress, Hagar fled into the desert. It is there she met God. The scriptures say that she gave this name to the Lord who spoke to her, "You are the God who sees me," for she said, "I have now seen the One who sees me" (Genesis 16:13).

He gave value to people who were excluded, outcast, and rejected.

And then there was a woman with no name: desperate, alone, discouraged, rejected, and forgotten.

And a woman was there who had been subject to bleeding for twelve years, but no one could heal her. She came up behind him and touched the edge of his cloak, and immediately her bleeding stopped.

"Who touched me?" Jesus asked.

When they all denied it, Peter said, "Master, the people are crowding and pressing against you."

But Jesus said, "Someone touched me; I know that power has gone out from me."

Then the woman, seeing that she could not go unnoticed, came trembling and fell at his feet. In the presence of all the people, she told why she had touched him and how she had been instantly

healed. Then he said to her, "Daughter, your faith has healed you. Go in peace."
LUKE 8:43-48

In the end, Jesus saw her, healed her, and called her daughter.

God calls us by name.

Names in the Bible are important, and so is yours. Being called by name tells you that your life matters. It builds a bridge of connection and makes the anonymous known. Acknowledging someone's name removes the power imbalance by flattening the hierarchy. When God calls someone by name, it changes his or her identity. Consider how Jacob came to be called Israel. After wrestling all night with a mysterious man, who he later discovered was God, he insisted on a blessing.

But Jacob replied, "I will not let you go unless you bless me."

The man asked him, "What is your name?"

"Jacob," he answered.

Then the man said, "Your name will no longer be Jacob, but Israel, because you have struggled with God and with humans and have overcome."

Jacob said, "Please tell me your name."

But he replied, "Why do you ask my
name?" Then he blessed him there.

So Jacob called the place Peniel, saying, "It is
because I saw God face to face, and yet my life
was spared."
GENESIS 32:26b-30

Later in Isaiah, the significance of this moment in
Jacob's life and in the life of his descendants is further
clarified. Names have power and create connection.

But now, this is what the LORD says-- he who
created you, O Jacob, he who formed you, O
Israel: "Do not fear, for I have redeemed you; I
have summoned you by name; you are mine."
ISAIAH 43:1

No human can truly fulfill his or her innate need to be
seen. But it is our calling as ministry leaders and pastors
to help people know the God who sees them and knows
their name.

How do we see others online?

"No one belongs here more than you." —Brené Brown

There is a huge difference between streaming your sermon online and building an online community. Streaming content is a one-way conversation. Building community online is a two-way dialogue. It's more than posting videos and sermons on Facebook or your website. That is "church TV." Instead, it requires a relationship. Building community online will take time and intention, just as it does in person.

Have you read Mary Schaller and John Crilly's book, *9 Arts of Spiritual Conversations*? This is one of those resources I keep going back too. Everyone on our team has a copy, and we have gone through the book as a series with our Pursuit Church Live online community. Here is an overview of 9 things you can do to build relationship and community online and in person.[3]

Art 1: Noticing

Author and Theologian, Frederick Buechner writes, "If we are to love our neighbors, before doing anything else we must see our neighbors. With our imagination as well as our eyes, that is to say like artists, we must see not just their faces but the life behind and within their faces. Here it is love that is the frame we see them in."

Jesus noticed people!

He not only sought out his neighbor, he saw them through his Father's eyes. People full of potential and hope. According to Dictionary.com, the action verb *to seek* means: "to go in search of, to try to find or discover by search or questioning."

Jesus raising a widow's son from the dead is a great example of noticing.

> Soon afterward, Jesus went to a town called
> Nain, and his disciples and a large crowd went
> along with him. As he approached the town
> gate, a dead person was being carried out—the
> only son of his mother, and she was a widow.
> And a large crowd from the town was with her.
> When the Lord saw her, his heart went out to
> her and he said, "Don't cry."
> LUKE 7:11-13

So noticing doesn't just mean seeing someone but seeking them out and discovering them with eyes of love and compassion. One practical way we can notice people online is by calling them by name during a live or in the comments.

Art 2: Praying

Richard Foster points to the value of praying for others, when he states, "If we truly love people, we will desire for them far more than it is within our power to give them, and this will lead to prayer."[4]

Jesus showed us this example when he prayed: "My prayer is not only for them (those that believe) but also for those who will believe through their message" (John 17:20).

Acts 2 describes the early church this way, "They devoted themselves to the apostles' teaching and to fellowship, to the breaking of break and to prayer...and the Lord added to their numbers daily those who were being saved" (Acts 2:42, 47b).

We can pray for people online by setting up a private prayer room and leading a live time of prayer on Facebook or other social networks.

Art 3: Listening

Let me ask you, would you rather be preached at or have someone get to know you by listening to your heart? I think most of us would prefer to know that someone is listening to our heart. ***Listening gives people what they need to feel safe and enter into relationship.***

James 1:19 says, "My dear brothers and sisters, take note of this: Everyone should be quick to listen, slow to speak, and slow to become angry."

Hearing is an auditory process, but listening involves the whole person. There are several key benefits to listening. When I listen:

- I create space for a trusting relationship.
- I grow in self-control, making the other person more important than myself.
- I stop stealing stories, e.g., interrupting and taking control.
- I show the person they are valued more than my opinion and agenda.
- I give people the space to discover their own answers.

We can connect with people online through active listening. Try using these phrases when responding to comments and messages: "What you are saying is important to me....," and "What I'm hearing is...," and "It sounds like you are saying...."

Art 4: Asking Questions

Good questions help people in the process of self-discovery and God-discovery. Henry Kimsey-House wrote, "When you are curious, you are no longer in the role of expert." Here are 5 characteristics of good questions you can use online.[5]

1. Like listening, good questions arise from curiosity and a genuine interest in another person.
2. Good questions are open ended. Use classic openers such as who, what, why, and how.
3. Good questions are concise.

4. Good questions are thoughtful. They connect with what is being discussed to move the conversation forward.
5. Good questions help people feel safe and understood.

Trust is the bridge that can bear the weight of truth. Trust is built when others see and feel your genuine interest in their lives and opinions.[6]

Art 5: Loving

We love God by loving others.

Knowing God changes us. As Colossians 3:14 instructs, "...over all these virtues put on love (agape), which binds them all together in perfect unity." When we experience and know God's compassion and hope for our lives, His love rips out our self-absorption and replaces it with a powerful love for others. We begin to see others through the eyes of God instead of our own eyes, even those who live differently than us.

Jesus said, "Love the lord your God with all your heart and with all your soul and with all your mind. This is the first and greatest commandment. And second is like it: Love your neighbor as yourself" (Matthew 22:37–40).

Love is not only a feeling it is an action! God has shown this in the way He loves us. In Romans 5:8, we learn that "God demonstrated his own love for us in this: while we were still sinners, Christ dies for us."

God loved us before we ever chose Him. That is a life-changing gift we can give to others. Author and theologian Elton Trueblood wrote, "What we need is not intellectual theorizing or even preaching, but a demonstration. One of the most powerful ways of turning people's loyalty to Christ is by loving others with the great love of God."[7]

Love shows up.

We love people online the way Jesus loved in person. He met each person with acceptance, service, healing, and teaching. To love people online, means to set aside our judgment of who we think people are or who we think they should be, and instead remember that acceptance leads to relationship, relationship leads to trust, and trust leads to an openness to God's help and salvation.

Art 6: Welcoming

The Rule of Saint Benedict, written around c. 480 – 550 AD, gave instructions to the monks on how to live communally. Chapter 53 is dedicated to teaching on the reception of guests.[8]

Let all guests who arrive be received like Christ, for He is going to say, "I came as a guest, and you received Me" (Matthew 25:35).

Welcoming is one powerful way of putting the spiritual gift of hospitality into practice. According to Henri Nouwen, "Hospitality, therefore, means primarily the creation of a free space where the stranger can enter and become a friend instead of an enemy."[9]

Welcoming is a way of living.[10] We often think of "welcoming" as inviting people into our home or our church, expecting people to come to us. This was true for the monks living at the monastery, and it can be true for us as well. But Jesus gave us a different example as he traveled and ministered to others.

In the story of the woman at the well, in John chapter 4, we read: "Now [Jesus] had to go through Samaria." In a Jewish culture that shunned Samaritans, many Jews chose to avoid Samaria. However, Jesus purposely went through it and met the woman at the well. He knew every detail of this woman's dark past but still extended unconditional acceptance and compassion. Jesus' act of welcoming changed this woman's understanding of herself and made her the first disciple in Samaria. The scriptures tell us the woman RAN back to her town to tell everyone about Jesus!

I am personally challenged by this example of Jesus. This makes me ask myself the question: Is the reflection of Jesus so vivid in my life that it sends people running to tell their friends how different life can be when you know Him?

One practical way we can welcome people online is by recruiting a care team of online engagers who connect with people by sharing posts and dialoging with others in comments and messenger.

Art 7: Facilitating

As Christian leaders, we believe one of the best ways people learn is by engaging in dialogue with their peers. This principle is established in Proverbs 27:17 (NLT), where it says, "As iron sharpens iron, so a friend sharpens a friend." Therefore, church is more than staring at the back of the head of the person in front of us, as we all watch the people on stage lead worship and preach. Instead, we are edified by one another in community through dialogue.

Mark and I raised our kids in two incredible churches. The worship was done with excellence, the kid's programs were entertaining, and the pastors were dynamic. The problem for me was the car ride home. I would ask, "What did you learn today?" or "What stood out to you in the message?" Inevitably, my kids would say, "Love Jesus." This is not a bad answer, but it frustrated me. I wondered what I was doing wrong. How could I help my kids know

Jesus beyond the song, "Jesus loves me?" How could I teach them to integrate their faith into everyday life?

When we asked our kids how we could make this different, my oldest son had an insightful response, "I want to study the Bible in a small group." Our church saw this need as well. It wasn't long before the large gathering of students was invited to join small group Bible studies.

What my son wanted was a facilitator NOT a teacher. This is a flipped style of learning that changes the role of the teacher from "sage on the stage" to a "guide on the side."[11] Facilitating gives every person in the group equal importance in discovering the answers. Each person is afforded the opportunity to reflect, dialogue, and be transformed in the company of community.

Tim Keller says, "We sought to mine the riches of the material as a community, assuming together we would see far more than any individual could."[12]

We can achieve the art of facilitating online by starting small groups using Facebook groups, Zoom, or the Bible App. There are many options to meet the needs of your specific congregation.

Art 8: Serving

Most people will not decide to follow Jesus due to our persuasive arguments. Instead, they will meet Jesus when we serve them or serve with them, like Jesus did.

Jesus served alone, e.g., washing the feet of the disciples. He also served with others, e.g., feeding the great crowds loaves and fishes. Yet, Jesus had a more profound purpose in mind than just clean feet and full bellies. Both illustrations of serving were significant teachable moments and faith building experiences for his disciples and those they served.

Serving together not only impacts the people we serve, we too are restored as we serve others. As Proverbs 11:25 says, "A generous person will prosper; whoever refreshes others will be refreshed."

Here are some of the many benefits of serving I have experienced myself and witnessed in others:

- Enhances contentment
- Reduces stress
- Takes your focus off yourself
- Boosts your mood
- Builds confidence
- Gives you a purpose beyond yourself
- Bonds you with others

Serving answers some of life's biggest questions: How do I make a difference in the world? Where do I find meaning and purpose?

This passage, from The Message translation, helps answer this question.

Let me tell you why you are here. You're here to be salt-seasoning that brings out the God-flavors of this earth. If you lose your saltiness, how will people taste godliness? You've lost your usefulness and will end up in the garbage. Here's another way to put it: You're here to be light, bringing out the God-colors in the world. God is not a secret to be kept. We're going public with this, as public as a city on a hill. If I make you light-bearers, you don't think I'm going to hide you under a bucket, do you? I'm putting you on a light stand. Now that I've put you there on a hilltop, on a light stand—shine! Keep open house; be generous with your lives. By opening up to others, you'll prompt people to open up with God, this generous Father in heaven.

MATTHEW 5:13-16, THE MESSAGE

Church online is the gateway to including people who have been on the sidelines of your church, unable to serve. Begin to ask God, "Who has been left out?" Most of our volunteers at Pursuit Church Live were passionate believers before finding us online but unable to serve due to schedules, chronic illness, location, education, or age. Church online gives everyone the opportunity to serve.

Church online is also the bridge to serving our members and communities in person. We start by identifying the needs of our communities, neighborhoods, or workplaces. And then we set up care teams to serve. (See part III for more information about setting up care teams.)

Art 9: Sharing

What compels us to share?

Love.

When we have experienced the true power of the gospel message, we will feel compelled to share the grace and freedom we have found in Jesus. This is why the message of Jesus and salvation is called the "good news!" As Luke 2:10 says, "…the good news will bring great joy to *all* people."

I want all people to know the love, joy, peace, compassion, grace, and acceptance I have found in my relationship with Christ. Don't you?

We can share online by teaching our online community how to share. Here are some ideas:

1. **Becoming a new creation in Christ.** Knowing Him should change us. Jesus said when we know Him we will become a "new creation" (2 Corinthians 5:17). As we study the scriptures and

37

learn who Jesus is and how he treated people, it will change how we act. People will begin to notice your old habits disappearing and new ones developing!

2. **Sharing our stories.** Stories change our minds. They break the silence and bring hope. In fact, approximately seventy-five percent of scripture consists of narrative, fifteen percent is expressed in poetic forms, and only ten percent is propositional and overtly instructional in nature.[13]

3. **Sharing God's Story.** When someone sees you change and hears your story, they will begin to ask you, "Why are you different?" First Peter 3:15 says, "Always be prepared to give an answer to everyone who asks you to give the reason for the hope that you have. *But do this with gentleness and respect.*" Take note of that last part. The first and most important reason to share your faith in Jesus should always be your genuine love for the other person, not obligation or personal agenda.[14] Telling God's story should by framed in prayer, take less than a minute, and never be a lecture.

Enock's story

Enock came to PCL by the invitation of a friend he went to church with in Kampala, Uganda. As a young boy, Enock lost his father and had to drop out of school to help support his family. Since I have known Enock, he has also lost his mother to illness, leaving him and his brother as orphans. These circumstances could lead someone to depression, drugs, gangs, or worse but not Enock. God gave Enock a passion for photography and storytelling. Through the help of one of our partner churches in his local community, Enock was able to borrow professional camera equipment to walk out his calling. Enock now works in the media department for that church and is a successful freelance photographer in Kampala. Here is a note I received from Enock the first time I posted his photograph and story:

Thanks miss Angela
I just saw the posts
Am so very humbled
Now the world knows I exist.
Thank you

Wow this has really inspired me more
Knowing that there's someone who cares about this boy.
Thanks Angela
This is giving me reason to push on and never to give up.
Thanks for the Love

Friends, this is how we see people online. This is how we build community.

PART II:

DISCIPLE

They joined with the other believers and devoted themselves to the apostles' teaching and fellowship sharing in the Lord's Supper and in prayer. A deep sense of awe came over them all, and the apostles performed many miraculous signs and wonders. And all the believers met together constantly and shared everything they had. They sold their possessions and shared the proceeds with those in need. They worshiped together at the Temple each day, met in homes for the Lord's Supper, and shared their meals with great joy and generosity — all the while praising God and enjoying the goodwill of all the people. And each day the Lord added to their group those who were being saved.

ACTS 2:42–47, NLT

Moving Discipleship Online

"A disciple is a person who has decided that the most important thing in their life is to learn how to do what Jesus said to do." —Dallas Willard

After the Day of Pentecost and the formation of the Early Church, God tells us which functions or purposes the church should focus on. Acts 2:42 says, "They devoted themselves to the apostles' teaching and to fellowship, to the breaking of bread and to prayer."

If there is one benefit of crisis, it is its ability to make priorities clear. In our current social state, church leaders are forced to recreate in-person community online.

Did you know more people have mobile devices than toothbrushes and grandparents are the fastest growing users on Twitter?[1] Adopting a social media strategy for your church is a matter of practicality. Online discipleship will require a mental shift from the norm of Sunday morning sermons and Wednesday night Bible studies, but it can be done with enormous success. Through social media, you can reach people everywhere, at any time.

Knowing your congregation is an important start to finding the right online platform. Do they have a phone? Do they have access to the internet? Are they using social networks? How digitally equipped are they? We know that 96% of Americans have cellphones and over 65% worldwide.[2] These numbers are growing by the minute. This makes discipleship online possible, even for those who are less technically equipped. Try these ideas:

1. **Create a Facebook group**. I don't recommend starting a Facebook group until you know your demographic and your specific purpose. The most popular Facebook groups (outside of fan pages for people and teams) are focused on meeting a need or bringing people together who have common interests. Ask yourself, what is the biggest need in

my church and local community? Could that need be met in a Facebook Group? For example, you can use Facebook groups to create a prayer room or invite your members to discuss your current sermon series. Facebook groups are also a great way to reach your local community. Start an "I love [your city name here]" group to share needed resources and promote volunteerism for your local community. Make sure to choose the appropriate privacy settings for your group. For example, if you plan to use Facebook groups for a members-only prayer room, please make your group private. If your church intends to start a Facebook group to serve your local community, make your group public in the settings tab on your group page.

2. **Organize your small groups using a face-to-face online service like Zoom or Microsoft teams.** If you have never used video conference call programs before, this option will surprise and encourage you. Most video conferencing companies offer several levels and options to meet the needs of your small groups. For example, Zoom has a free service for meetings 40 minutes or less. It is user friendly and has the option for people without video capabilities to phone into your meeting.

3. **Equip members for one-to-one discipleship** via phone, email, FaceTime, or a social media messenger system. As pastors and ministry leaders, it is our job to make disciples who make disciples. At Pursuit Church Live, we have a phrase you will hear often: *Who's your one?* Our challenge is for every Christ-follower to have one person they pray for and read the Bible with.

4. **Utilize the amazing gift of the free YouVersion Bible App.** The YouVersion Bible App is a great tool for helping your church attenders engage every day with God's Word. One feature of the Bible App is called Plans with Friends, which allows people to work through the same plan together and discuss it right inside the app.[3] The Bible App also allows friends to pray for one another. The YouVersion Bible App is a great tool for groups and for one-to-one discipleship. This year at Pursuit Church Live, we are inviting our church community to read the New Testament together using the YouVersion Bible App. The reflections, dialogue, and change I see in those who are following the plan has been more than I could have ever imagined.

Understanding Social Learning

"We live in a digital ecosystem, and it is vital that educational institutions adapt." —Carla Dawson, Digital Marketing Professor at the Catholic University of Cordoba

One of the biggest challenges pastors face is getting people to come to church beyond Sunday. In the 2020 "Barna: State of the Church" research, we see church attendance on a steady decline.[4] The surprising ray of hope in this study is that consistent Bible reading has remained steady over the last decade. Social networks give churches the opportunity of a lifetime: the opportunity to come together for daily Bible study and prayer.

Before creating content, we need to understand how social networks are changing the way we consume information and the way we learn. According to digital learning expert, Eloise Peterson, "Attention spans both in school and at work are decreasing." A study conducted by Microsoft found that, due to our increasingly digital lifestyles, people have shorter attention spans than goldfish. The study surveyed 2,000 participants and found that while they could multitask at great lengths, their attention span had fallen to an average of eight seconds. A goldfish's attention span is nine seconds.[5]

Most of us understand this shift because we have felt like goldfish at one point or another. But all is not lost. As a student of organizational leadership at Gonzaga and now an online professor at Northwest University, I have witnessed the power of digital learning environments, but it requires a pivot in your teaching style. To be successful online communicators and teachers, we must shift from an instructor-led model to an instructor-less model of teaching. An instructor-less style clearly articulates the main point of the lesson while adopting a pedagogy approach of teaching that provides for purposeful interaction among the community you lead. Online, this begins with micro-moments.

Research has shown teaching in micro-moments to be an effective way for instructors to capture attention and for students to retain information. That is important when we think of online discipleship opportunities. Microlearning comes in bite-sized, easy to digest pieces of information that happen in text, images, videos, audio clips, or polls.

Did Jesus teach in micro-moments?

"Follow me…" —Jesus

There are six ways I see Jesus use microlearning to disciple and teach others.

1. **Jesus used short stories.** Mark 4:34 says, "He did not speak to them without a parable, but privately to his own disciples he explained everything." Jesus spoke in parables to make a point and teach

us how to live. Sharing short stories online is a powerful way to teach the Bible in micro-moments.

2. **Jesus asked questions**. Instead of telling people the answer, Jesus often asked questions, 307 of them to be exact.[6] Jesus knew questions opened the door to self-discovery and understanding. Questions empower the listener or reader to seek answers. Questions show others you are interested in what they think. Questions are an important part of creating opportunity for those who are exploring faith online.

3. **Jesus created memorable phrases.** A great example is the golden rule found in Luke 6:31, "Do to others as you would have them do to you." These sayings make great sharable graphics and teaching opportunities.

4. **Jesus made bold statements.** The truth is, Jesus liked to shock people with hyperbole language. For example, in Matthew 5:29-30, Jesus doesn't pull any punches when he declares, "If your right eye causes you to stumble, gouge it out and throw it away. It is better for you to lose one part of your body than for your whole body to be thrown into hell. And if your right hand causes you to stumble, cut it off and throw it away. It is better for

you to lose one part of your body than for your whole body to go into hell." Sharing these surprisingly bold statements of Jesus online can grab people's attention and create interesting dialogue among followers.

5. **Jesus used repetition.** Jesus taught specific themes. For example, Jesus talks about money in 11 out of 39 parables.[7] In the fast paced world of digital ministry, repetition holds an important key to unlocking the truths of the Bible for the people you serve.

6. **Jesus taught by practical demonstration.** The washing of the disciples' feet was an object lesson demonstrated by Jesus to teach servant leadership. Teaching by practical application is crucial in equipping your online community. At PCL, we use demonstration to teach people how to take communion or how to baptize others when they are unable to attend church in person.

Building your online team

So Christ himself gave the apostles, the
prophets, the evangelists, the pastors and
teachers, to equip his people for works of service, so
that the body of Christ may be built up until we all
reach unity in the faith and in the knowledge of the

Son of God and become mature, attaining to the whole measure of the fullness of Christ."
EPHESIANS 4:11-13

Jesus had a unique way of making disciples who made disciples. He used a mentorship/apprentice method similar to the commonly used five-step leadership development model below.[8]

1. I do. You watch. We talk.
2. I do. You help. We talk.
3. You do. I help. We talk.
4. You do. I watch. We talk.
5. You do. Someone else watches.

More often than not, I find people in the church want to serve but need help having obstacles removed. The first obstacle is time. Unlike most brick-in-mortar churches, the door of online churches is open 24 hours a day, 7 days a week. Having church online brings with it enormous potential for equipping the people of your church for service.

Our churches are currently full of social equity sitting on the sidelines. My advice is look for people whose life makes it impossible to get to church every Sunday. People like the single dad who works two jobs, the woman with chronic illness, the young adult without experience, or the retired gentleman who doesn't know where he fits in. The second obstacle is the myth that a person needs a title or

Bible degree to serve and disciple others. This was not the way Jesus made disciples, and it shouldn't be the way we disciple. Jane Bozarth, author of "Social Media for Trainers," puts it this way, "We complain that learners want to be spoon-fed, but then we won't let them hold the spoon."[9]

At PCL, we emphatically believe that every person plays a role in telling the story of Jesus with their life. There is no one in this world without influence. In person, that influence starts with your family and works its way into your neighborhood, job, community, and beyond. Online influence begins with friends and followers. It is our church's mission to make everyone aware of his or her personal circle of influence. And, as a community, we are committed to making Jesus the center of social media.

AnnaStina's Story

For the first time in my adult life I was what I called a "pew sitter." Someone who just showed up to church, heard the message, and went home. I was depressed. REALLY depressed. I was on the verge of giving up. Obviously, God had heard my prayers, but he had nothing for me. I really was 50 and useless. April 3, 2018. The day and week that I was proven SO wrong. God DID have something for me. Something AMAZING for me. Just as I was about to give up HE shows up BIG time! How you might ask? Well, He showed up through a Pastor whose name is Angela Craig. I had been watching online services and praise and worship on a site that I had no idea was connected to anyone or any group I had already known. HOWEVER, she was watching me. I received a message from her asking me how could she get me more plugged in at Pursuit Church Live. She had NO idea at the time that she was answering prayers. Many, many prayers. I sat in my living room in tears and my husband looked over at me and asked what was wrong... NOTHING! NOTHING was wrong, everything was RIGHT. We talked and I asked her for prayer and on April 3rd she asked if I would be interested in coming on board with PCL. More tears.... pure tears of happiness, joy, excitement. YES, YES, and again I say YES! Within a week I was asked if I would like to take on more with PCL. YES! She saw value in me and soon I was submerged in everything PCL. I met amazing people from all over and when I say ALL over I mean ALL over! Even in Uganda! I feel alive again. My joy has returned. I was ready to give up!

PART III:

CARE

And they continued steadfastly in the apostles' doctrine and fellowship, and in breaking of bread, and in prayers. And fear came upon every soul: and many wonders and signs were done by the apostles. And all that believed were together, and had all things common; and sold their possessions and goods, and parted them to all men, as every man had need. And they, continuing daily with one accord in the temple, and breaking bread from house to house, did eat their meat with gladness and singleness of heart, Praising God, and having favour with all the people. And the Lord added to the church daily such as should be saved.

ACTS 2:42-47, KJV

Caring for Community Online and Beyond

"Church is not a building; it's a people." —Nona Jones

You must have a "care strategy" not only for your church but also for yourself. Just like the flight attendant instructs at the beginning of every flight, it's advisable to put your oxygen mask on before assisting others. As one pastor told me in his second week of digital ministry, "I have only been a social media pastor for one week and I am exhausted!"

In my book, *Pivot Leadership: Small Steps...Big Change,* I wrote a chapter titled "The Art of Inaccessibility" in which I discuss boundaries and self-care for the mind, body, and soul. In leadership, boundaries are essential. Boundaries sustain and boundaries inspire. The former Prime Minister of Great Britain and Northern Ireland, Tony Blair, said, "The art of leadership is not saying *yes*, it is saying *no*."[1] "Yes" can be hazardous for several reasons. Overcommitting and being accessible to the needs of others 24/7 can be dangerous to our minds, our bodies, our souls, and our families.

Through numerous studies, The American Institute of Stress states the demands of work as the number one cause of stress and work-life imbalance which leads to disease, depression, anxiety, loss of sleep, and a decline in productivity and purpose.[2] Jesus asked, "...what do you benefit if you gain the whole world but lose your own soul? Is anything worth more than your soul?" (Matthew 16:26, NLT). Living in a boundless existence of "yeses" can cause us to lose our focus on what matters most in life (following Jesus and loving others), and it can clearly be a detriment to our mind, body, and soul.[3]

What does your heart need? This question is where care begins. Here are my top three steps for personal care:

Step 1: *Margin* (Attending to the mind)

"A life lived without borders is a life lived in captivity"
—Todd Stocker

Being an online pastor will challenge your boundaries. But there is something you can do about it. Margin makes us smarter, more creative, and productive. Take a look at your to-do list and calendar—do you have adequate margin to give your best to community? These questions may help:

- ✓ *Do the commitments on my calendar match my personal, family, and/or organizational mission and vision?*
- ✓ *What is my motivation for committing to each of the items on my calendar?*
- ✓ *Have I left margin in my schedule to attend to an unexpected need or opportunity?*
- ✓ *Who can I empower and delegate responsibility to?*

Step 2: *Rest, diet, and exercise* (Attending to the body)

"Self-care is never a selfish act - it is simply good stewardship of the only gift I have, the gift I was put on earth to offer others. Anytime we can listen to true self and give the care it requires, we do it not only for

ourselves, but for the many others whose lives we touch." —Parker Palmer

Why is the area of self-care (rest, diet, and exercise) least attended to by leaders? Twenty pounds of extra weight, an unused membership to the gym, and a bottle of sleeping pills are not uncommon realities for church leaders. As a lead pastor, I understand what it's like to put everyone else's needs before your own. Sadly, our bodies are not as dismissive of rest, exercise, and a healthy diet as we are. At some point we will pay the price for our neglect. Significant change begins by making small changes. Maybe that small change is as simple as putting your phone on Do Not Disturb between the hours of 10pm – 6am or taking a 15 minute walk each day at lunch. Small things done in repetition create big change. Start here:

✓ *What small change in your sleep, diet, or exercise can you make today that will reward you tomorrow?*

Step 3: *Replenish-restore-remember* (Attending to the Soul)

"To keep a lamp burning, we must put oil in it."
—Mother Teresa

Leaders can hold on to busyness like a weapon of protection. However, without a time to replenish and restore, our souls wither. Sometimes we avoid our need for soul care because we are afraid of what we will find. Don't do it! You have witnessed what happens to pastors who avoid self-care. Disengagement, lethargy, frustration, guilt, insecurity, and a loss of vision are the smallest consequences of an unattended soul. Even bigger consequences threaten to destroy your witness and impact for God. Remember the advice in 1 Peter 5:8, "Stay alert! Watch out for your great enemy, the devil. He prowls around like a roaring lion, looking for someone to devour (NLT).

Leaders need time to unplug. Leaders need a time of refueling. Leaders need time to remember *Who* called them and what they are called to. Whether you call it retreat, wilderness, solitude, or meditation, leaders need to stop and be with God in order to pour themselves out to others.

✓ *Review your calendar. Have you scheduled time to care for your soul?*

Developing Care Teams

"Caring for 30 people personally is possible. Caring for 230 is not. Many pastors burn out trying."
—Carey Nieuwhof

God never designed the church for one person to be the answer for everyone's problems. But, today, most churches have one person in charge of pastoral care—the lead pastor. Unfortunately, this is not scalable or practical in a time of crisis *or* anytime. As ministry leaders, we care for ourselves and we care for others when we empower and equip "care teams" to serve.

A worldwide pandemic, deaths, births, celebrations, illness, emotional crisis, and parenting or marriage counseling can all be broken into three categories: *emergency, counseling, or encouragement.* Creating care teams for each of these categories, built on simple systems of function, communication, and team building, will address both your short-term and long-term needs.

Emergency Care Teams:

Emergencies are things can't anticipate or fully plan for. Your emergency care team serves as the first responders to crisis. Earthquakes, tornadoes, pandemics, death, disability, and hospitalization are all examples of crises that fall within the category of emergency.

Practical Tips for Emergency Care Teams

- ✓ Look for team members who are known to show up in the event of an emergency with help, love, and compassion.
- ✓ Create communication procedures and guidelines for first responders (e.g., establish how many days an emergency care team member

should follow-up on a widow after the death of a spouse.)

✓ Assign a team to review social media daily for people who might find themselves in unexpected crisis. (Social media is an excellent tool to access the needs of your members and community.)

✓ Set up a helpline for your church and community (e.g., use technology like Google Voice to create a general phone number that will connect the person in need of emergency care to a team volunteer.)

✓ Create an administrative process for sending condolences, providing meals or supplies in a time of need.

Counseling Care Teams:

Counseling teams are set up to respond to short and long-term coaching needs for emotional crisis, parenting help, marital counseling, or addiction.

Practical Tips for Counseling Care Teams

✓ Procure a professional team of counselors to list on your website who are available to respond within 24 hours.

✓ Consider hosting small group programs at your church, (e.g., AA, Celebrate Recovery, Financial Peace Academy, pre-marital group counseling, or a parenting class), which would serve both people inside and outside the church.

✓ Consistently post counseling care classes and opportunities on your social media pages inviting your congregation and your local community to join.

Encouragement Care Teams:

Encouragers are people who naturally speak life into others: they celebrate, they pray, and they help in non-emergency situations.

Practical Tips for Encouragement Care Teams

✓ Establish a protocol for cards, gifts, or meals for a new birth, child dedications, baptism, illness, single parents, etc.

✓ Create an opportunity for intercessory prayer. You can do this in person or create a private online group for community prayer.

✓ Develop an online encourager team that interacts with people on your social media accounts.

✓ Consider assigning each encourager a group of people to call, email, or message for a weekly check-in.

Here is an example of how you could structure care teams:[4]

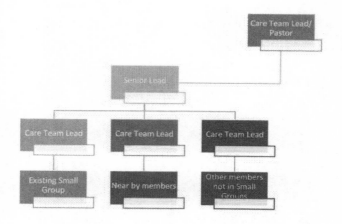

For these and any volunteer teams, have a training, communication, and recognition strategy to equip keep your volunteers engaged.

For centuries, the Church has been the first responders in sorrow and in joy. Exceptional leaders are those who empower the saints to love others and serve them the way Jesus taught us.

A new command I give you: Love one another. As
I have loved you, so you must love one
another. By this everyone will know that you are
my disciples, if you love one another.
JOHN 13:34-35, NIV

Difference Maker Project at Pursuit Church Live

When I started Pursuit Church Live, I had no idea we would become a global community overnight. The needs of an international community are enormous. Food, education, medical care, and the need for work are just a few of the requests we get on a daily basis. We discovered quickly that caring for the people of Pursuit would require a different strategy than what works for a conventional church.

Today, we have a two-fold strategy for serving the needs of our community. First, we connect PCL members to needed resources by partnering with on-the-ground nonprofit organizations in their local communities. Second, we raise awareness and funds for these partner organizations by donating all the church tithes and offerings we receive to one vetted non-profit organization each month through our Difference Maker Project.

With the help of our Difference Maker community, PCL was able to donate to the following organizations in 2019:

Khan Academy

Convoy of Hope

Women's Empowerment

Wounded Warrior Family Foundation

Doctors Without Borders

His Heart Foundation

Every Mom Counts

Cure International

The Hope House

People often ask me how we are able to donate all church tithes and offerings to the Difference Maker Project. This would not be possible if I pastored a traditional church with a building and staff. The minimal cost of doing church online and the generosity of our volunteer team to work for free allows us to care for our community in ways not available to a brick-and-mortar church. These are the kind of new opportunities church online can bring you and the people you care for.

PART IV:

PRACTICAL TIPS FOR CHURCH ONLINE

Boundaries

Social networks don't sleep, but you will need to. Establishing boundaries for you and your team will be essential for the longevity of your online church. Here are some practical ideas:

- ✓ **Turn off notifications to social networks.** You can do this by going to the "settings" icon on your phone and selecting "notifications."
- ✓ **Set your phone to "Do Not Disturb"** during Bible study, family time, and while you sleep.
- ✓ **Create a schedule.** Schedule specific time during the day and week to post and respond on social media.
- ✓ **Don't compare.** Don't be tempted to do something just because you see others doing it. Begin where your people are already gathering. In most cases, this will be Facebook.
- ✓ **Simplify!** Social networks are replacing blogs and websites. The less time you spend as a social media administrator, the more time you can be with your people.
- ✓ **Protect you, your team, and those you serve.** Consult your legal counsel to create a social media check-list/contract for you and your team to sign. An example can also be found under the "Digital Ministry Training" tab on my website at: www.angelalcraig.com

✓ **Update your insurance.** Connect with your local insurance agent to make sure your policy covers your online ministry and protects you, your team, and your board from personal liability.

Live Streaming

I recommend streaming with Facebook Live instead of other streaming services for 90% of the churches I consult with. There are four reasons for this:

✓ **Expense.** Even with the gift of free streaming services like Church Online Network or OBS, your church will need production equipment estimated at $4000 - $10,000 dollars. That doesn't include monthly expenses for staff and other incidentals.

✓ **Social capital.** If you have the budget, learning curve stamina, a large production crew, and an online hospitality team, streaming may be a great option. But most churches do not. Facebook makes it so easy to go live. You can do it on your own or enlist one or two volunteers to help you. This is a great opportunity to empower and equip the next generation in ministry and cultivate untapped talent.

✓ **Time commitment.** Building an online community takes time and investment. People need you not a fancy video of you. Choose people over production.

✓ **Relationship vs. Church TV.** There is a place and a need for high quality Christian videos. But God did not call us to be famous, He called us to make Him famous. Think about this for a moment: Do you have a famous person you follow? What would you think if that person went live on Facebook to have a one-on-one conversation with you? What if they called you by name? What if he or she asked your opinion? How would it change your commitment? How would it change your relationship?

Tips for Facebook

✓ **Create a Facebook page.** Think of this as the yellow pages for your church and the front door to faith for people in your community not connected to a local body of believers.

✓ **Create Facebook groups** around specific needs or topics of interest, e.g., a private prayer group, a women's Bible study group, or a community service group.

✓ **Be consistent** with posts and brand. Use a free scheduling service like Buffer or Hootsuite to help you. You can create a brand template with colors and font styles in graphic apps like Spark from Adobe. There are also many Facebook pages and organizations like CV Outreach that share free graphics. Check out the full list of resources at my website: angelalcraig@pursuitchurchlive.com.

✓ **Use a language of invitation** that includes everyone you hope to reach. Try to avoid using "Christianese." Ask someone outside the church to give you feedback on your posts.

Going Live on Facebook

✓ **Practice.** Talking to yourself instead of a live audience takes some getting used to. In addition, technology is a gift, but it is not perfect. Regardless of how many times you have gone live before, always test your equipment, lighting, sound, Wi-Fi, and Facebook.

✓ **Hook first, intro second.** Open with a hook. Give the viewer a reason to stay. Tell them why this talk is relevant and helpful for them. Second, welcome everyone who is watching live and on replay. Ask them to comment and share by letting you know where they are watching from.

✓ **Don't time stamp your video.** Not only do people from all over the world have access to your video, many will replay it at different times of the day.

✓ **Recruit a hospitality team** to monitor comments and share your video to groups when you are live.

This team is responsible for welcoming people in the comments, asking questions, posting scriptures, and inviting viewers to get plugged in. They can also share your video to their personal pages and groups as a Watch Party.

✓ **Include viewers in your talk.** Make eye contact. Welcome them by name. Ask questions. Include their thoughts in your talk when appropriate.

✓ **Make a second welcome** and repeat the hook in the middle of your talk for those just tuning in.

✓ **Close with an invitation**: an invitation to know Jesus, an invitation to prayer, an invitation to join your community, etc. Give your viewers follow-up steps for accepting your invitation, e.g., an online connection card or a link to your prayer group.

✓ **Close with essential announcements.** I don't recommend opening with announcements. Make announcements via a post or an event on your Facebook page or group. Save what is important for the end and remember to ask people to share your video. I often say, "If this helped you, please share it."

✓ **Add captions**. Eighty-five percent of social media users scroll posts without the sound on. Adding captions after your video has processed will help engage and garner attention.

Communion

How have you experienced communion? For most, communion has been administered by a priest or ordained minister, steeped in traditions of prayer, rituals, symbolism, and even special clothes, cups, and bowls. Understandably, these experiences can make us feel uncomfortable with offering communion outside church walls. Let's look at the Bible for understanding and consider how the practice of communion can be integrated into church online.

- ✓ **What is the purpose of communion?** 1 Corinthians 11:23-26 explains the primary purpose of communion. Communion is a time to remember. It's an invitation to remember what Jesus has done for us. It is a time to worship and a time of gratitude in the presence of God for His forgiveness of our sins and the new life we have received in Jesus Christ. Additionally, 1 Corinthians 11:27-32 challenges us to a time of personal reflection and heart examination as we consider our relationship with God and others.
- ✓ **Who can take communion?** Any person who believes in Jesus for his or her salvation. The Bible does not list church membership as a requirement.
- ✓ **What are the elements of communion?** At the last supper, "Jesus took bread, and when he had

given thanks, he broke it and gave it to his disciples, saying, 'Take and eat; this is my body.' Then he took a cup, and when he had given thanks, he gave it to them, saying, 'Drink from it, all of you. This is my blood of the covenant, which is poured out for many for the forgiveness of sins'" (Matthew 6:26-28). These scriptures teach us that bread represents Christ's body and wine represents Christ's blood.

✓ **Do I have to use bread and wine?** Crackers, bagels, matzo, and grape juice are great substitutes. We recommend a non-alcoholic beverage so kids can participate. When we read the scriptures, we see clearly that communion is about the heart: we remember, we reflect, we give thanks, we confess, we forgive. Bring to the table whatever elements you have to offer.

✓ **Who can serve communion?** The Bible says we are a priesthood of believers (1 Peter 2:5-9). All believers share in Christ priestly status, flattening institutional hierarchy and eliminating class structure. This gives every believer (both male and female) the authority to serve communion.

✓ **What's the proper way to serve communion?** The Bible doesn't give us a specific way to serve communion. The early church served communion in their homes after a meal together (Matthew 26:26-29; Acts 2:42-46; 1 Corinthians 11:20-26). At PCL we like to create an environment for worship, reflection, and thanksgiving and read scriptures that remind us of Christ's death, burial and resurrection, e.g., 1 Corinthians 11:23-32.

Celebrating communion is an important part of every Christ-follower's growth and transformation. Church online gives us an incredible opportunity to teach every believer how to share in the celebration of communion.

Baptism

The great commission calls us to go out and make disciples and baptize them in the name of the Father, Son, and Holy Spirit (Matthew 28:19-20). Baptism is yet another opportunity "to equip the saints for the work of ministry, for building up the body of Christ" (Ephesians 4:12-16).

- ✓ **What is baptism?** Baptism is a physical display of what is going on in the heart and mind. It is a public declaration of faith in Jesus Christ and obedience to follow God's Word (Mark 16:16).
- ✓ **Who is allowed to baptize?** In the Bible, Jesus' followers baptized others. You do not have to be a pastor to baptize someone; you only need to be a believer.
- ✓ **Do baptisms need to take place in a church building?** In the book of Acts 8:26-40, we read about the Ethiopian Eunuch being baptized by Philip on the roadside, "As they traveled along

the road, they came to some water and the eunuch said, 'Look, here is water. What can stand in the way of my being baptized?'" Find the water closest to you. I have baptized people in a kiddie pool.

✓ **What do I teach believers to do and say during the baptism?** There isn't a set standard in the Bible about exactly what to say and do during a baptism, but here is an overview of what we teach at PCL. Keep everyone safe by making sure believers understand the physical requirements for dunking someone in the water. Before dunking, ask the person being baptized to share their testimony of faith. Ask them to repeat, "I believe that Jesus is the Christ," then pause and let them repeat the phrase, then say, "the son of the living God," and let them repeat, then continue, "and I accept Him as my Lord and Savior." Ask the person to plug his/her nose. With one hand on the person's back and one hand on his/her arms, begin to lower the person. As you dunk them, proclaim, "You were buried with Christ," and as you raise them up say, "you are raised to life" (Romans 6:4). Have a second person on hand to help the person out of the water. Celebrate!!

Imagine with me for a moment if every believer was sharing the gospel and baptizing people anytime and anywhere like community lakes, pools, and even bathtubs!

For a full list of church online tips, visit: www.angelalcraig.com.

EPILOGUE

"Unless you act when it feels too early, it's actually too late."[1] This is where we began, and this is where we'll end. Like other watershed events in history, Covid-19 has been the catalyst to innovation. We are seeing a rebirth of the church as thousands of people connect with churches online. This pandemic has awakened our hearts and renewed our vision. Covid-19 has reminded us that church is not a building, it is a people. When the pandemic subsides, it will be tempting to go back to the status quo. Don't cave to the temptation. We can't go back to doing things the same way. Church attendance and membership have declined drastically in the last two decades. In 1999, 70% of Americans attended church. Today, less than half of Americans are church members.[2]

God has given us the tools of social networks to build His kingdom through digital ministry. Church online will never replace in-person community, but it will strengthen the Church as we serve, disciple, and care for people online. Moving forward in the ever-changing digital age, we will need adaptive leaders who never waste a crisis or challenge; adaptive leaders who are able to respond to the ongoing changes of our environment; adaptive leaders who focus on the opportunities not the problems; adaptive leaders who remain attentive to the vision, simplifying the mission to meet the needs of the people they serve. I believe you are one of these adaptive leaders.

The journey of digital ministry goes far beyond this book. It is a journey better taken in a community of like-minded leaders. I invite you to join my Online Jesus community. Visit my website, www.onlinejesus.info, for real-time digital ministry training, coaching, and consulting.

NOTES

INTRODUCTION

1. Andy Crouch, Kurt Keilhacker, and Dave Blanchard, "Leading Beyond the Blizzard: Why Every Organization Is Now a Startup," Praxis Labs, 20 March 2020, https://journal.praxislabs.org/leading-beyond-the-blizzard-why-every-organization-is-now-a-startup-b7f32fb278ff.
2. Andrew Perrin and Monica Anderson, "Share of U.S. Adults Using Social Media, including Facebook, is mostly unchanged since 2018" Pew Research Center, 10 April 2019, https://www.pewresearch.org/fact-tank/2019/04/10/share-of-u-s-adults-using-social-media-including-facebook-is-mostly-unchanged-since-2018/.
3. Maryam Mohsin, "10 Facebook Stats Every Marketer Should Know in 2020," Oberlo, 3 December 2019, https://www.oberlo.com/blog/facebook-statistics
4. Posting by Facebook Newsroom, https://about.fb.com/news.
5. Research cited in video, https://www.facebook.com/groups/LifeChurchOnline.

PART I: COMMUNITY

1. "The Martyrdom of the Holy Martyrs Justin Martyr, Chariton, Charites, Paeon, and Liberianus," Christian History for Everyman, accessed 8 April 2020, https://www.christian-history.org/justin-martyr-martyrdom.html.
2. Tiia Tulviste Ph.D., Deborah L. Best Ph.D., and Judith L Gibbons Ph.D., Children's Social Worlds in Cultural Context (Cham, Switzerland: Springer, 2019), 91.
3. Mary Shaller and John Crilly, 9 Arts of Spiritual Conversations: Walking Alongside People Who Believe Differently (Chicago: Tyndale Momentum, 2016).
4. Schaller and Crilly, 57.
5. Schaller and Crilly, 99.
6. Schaller and Crilly, 111.
7. Excerpts from Trueblood, in Newby, The Best of Elton Trueblood.

8. "A hospitality lesson from Benectines: The Rule of Benedict on the Reception of Guests," Ephatta Blog, 28 September 2016, http://blog.ephatta.com/en/2016/09/28/a-hospitality-lesson-from-benectines-the-rule-of-benedict-on-the-reception-of-guests/.

9. Henri J. M. Nouwen, Spirituality and Practice: Resources for Spiritual Journeys, accessed 8 April 2020, https://www.spiritualityandpractice.com/quotes/quotations/view/10127/spiritual-quotation.

10. Schaller and Crilly, 139.

11. Schaller and Crilly, 159.

12. Schaller and Crilly, 168.

13. Colin Harbinson, Restoring the Arts to the Church: The Role of Creativity in the Expression of Truth, accessed April 6, 2020, https://www.colinharbinson.com/teaching/resthearts.html.

14. Schaller and Crilly, 197.

PART II: DISCIPLE

1. Alejandra Guzman, "6 Ways Social Media Is Changing the World," World Economic Forum, accessed April 9, 2020, http://weforum.org.

2. "Demographics of Mobile Devices," Pew Research Center, 12 June 2019, http://www.pewresearch.org/internet/fact-sheet/mobile/.

3. Can be accessed at: https://open.life.church/resources/3488-plans-with-friends.

4. "Barna: State of the Church," Barna, accessed April 10, 2020, https://www.barna.com/research/state-of-the-church-2020/.

5. "Canadians Now Have Shorter Attention Span than Goldfish Thanks to Portable Devices: Microsoft Study," National Post, 12 May 2015, http://www.nationalpost.com/news/canada/canadans-now-have-shorter-attention-span-than-goldfish-thanks-to-portable-devices-microsoft-study/amp

6. Martin B. Copenhaver, "Jesus Is the Question: the 307 Questions Jesus Asked and the 3 He Answered," (Abingdon Press, 2014).

7. Jeffrey Poor, "Jesus' Most Common Teaching Wasn't About Money," Relevant Media Group, 13 Nov. 2019, http://www.relevantmagazine.com.

8. Patrick O'Connell, "The 5 Steps of Leadership Development" Aspen Group, 26 June 2019, http://www.aspengroup.com.

9. Jane Bozarth, *Social Media for Trainers* (San Francisco, CA: Pfeiffer, 2010).

PART III: CARE

1. Angela Craig, Pivot Leadership: Small Steps…Big Change (Fall City: EiS Publishing, 2015), 34.

2. AIS , (2014) "Workplace Stress," Retrieved from The American Institute of Stress, http://www.stress.org/workplace-stress.

3. Angela Craig, 34.

4. Designed by Janet Richards, Redmond Assembly of God, Redmond, Washington.

EPILOGUE

1. Andy Crouch, Kurt Keilhacker, and Dave Blanchard, "Leading Beyond the Blizzard: Why Every Organization Is Now a Startup," Praxis Labs, 20 March 2020, https://journal.praxislabs.org/leading-beyond-the-blizzard-why-every-organization-is-now-a-startup-b7f32fb278ff.

2. Jeffrey M. Jones, "U.S. Church Membership Down Sharply in Past Two Decades," Gallup, 18 April 2019, https://news.gallup.com/poll/248837/church-membership-down-sharply-past-two-decades.aspx.

ABOUT THE AUTHOR

Angela Craig is the lead pastor of Pursuit Church Live, the first social media church in the Assemblies of God fellowship. Angela has a master's degree in organizational leadership and is a sought-after leadership coach and speaker, helping teams and organizations turn their online platforms into communities. Angela lives in Seattle, WA with her husband, Mark.

Made in the USA
Columbia, SC
10 September 2021